TIMELINE OF DUKE ELLINGTON'S LIFE

1899 Edward Kennedy "Duke" Ellington is born in Washington, D.C.

1907 Eight-year-old Edward takes piano lessons but has little interest in music.

1913 Edward suddenly becomes interested in playing the piano. He works hard to perfect his skills and writes his first music piece. A friend suggests Edward use the nickname "Duke."

1917 Duke Ellington leaves school to become a full-time musician. He forms his own band, and the next year marries his girlfriend, Edna Thompson.

1919 Duke's son, Mercer, is born.

1923 Duke moves to New York and joins a band in Harlem, a hot music spot.

1927 Duke and his band become known for their exciting new jazz sound. They get a chance to play in Harlem's most famous nightclub, The Cotton Club.

THIS WAY

1928 -1931 Duke and his band become a popular attraction at The Cotton Club. Their music is broadcast on the radio, and they record hit after hit. The band is now known as *Duke Ellington and his Orchestra*.

1933 By now, Duke Ellington and his orchestra are world famous. They tour Europe and play in cities all over the United States.

1943 Duke performs his first concert at New York's Carnegie Hall. It is the first of 25 times he will perform there during his career.

1956 Duke has a super-successful concert at the Newport Jazz Festival. He is featured on the cover of *Time* magazine.

1960 -1973 The orchestra makes tons of recordings and appearances. Duke composes some award-winning movie soundtracks as well.

1974 Duke Ellington dies in New York City at the age of seventy-five.

UP HERE

GETTING TO KNOW
THE WORLD'S
GREATEST COMPOSERS

D U K E
ELLINGTON

WRITTEN AND ILLUSTRATED BY MIKE VENEZIA

CONSULTANT
DONALD FREUND, PROFESSOR OF COMPOSITION,
INDIANA UNIVERSITY SCHOOL OF MUSIC

CHILDREN'S PRESS®

An Imprint of Scholastic Inc.

Picture Acknowledgements

Music on the cover, Stock Montage, Inc.; 3, The Bettmann Archive; 5, Victor Haboush; 11, AP/Wide World Photos; 12, Art and Artifacts Division, Schomburg Center for Research in Black Culture, The New York Public Library, Astor, Lenox and Tilden Foundation; 13, National Museum of American Art, Smithsonian Institution, Gift of the Harmon Foundation; 14-15, Frank Driggs Collection; 18, Culver Pictures, Inc.; 19, UP/Bettmann; 21, Frank Driggs Collection; 28, The Bettmann Archive; 31, © Duncan P. Schiedt; 32, AP/Wide World Photos

Colorist for interior illustrations: Kathy Hickey

Library of Congress Cataloging-in-Publication Data

Names: Venezia, Mike, author, illustrator.
Title: Duke Ellington / written and illustrated by Mike Venezia.
Description: Revised edition. | New York : Children's Press, 2017. | Series: Getting to know the world's greatest composers | Includes bibliographical references and index.
Identifiers: LCCN 2017022722| ISBN 9780531226582 (library binding : alk. paper) | ISBN 9780531230367 (pbk. : alk. paper)
Subjects: LCSH: Ellington, Duke, 1899-1974--Juvenile literature. | Jazz musicians--United States--Biography--Juvenile literature.
Classification: LCC ML3930.E44 V46 2017 | DDC 781.65092 [B] --dc23 LC record available at https://lccn.loc.gov/2017022722

1 2 3 4 5 6 7 8 9 10 R 27 26 25 24 23 22 21 20 19 18

Duke Ellington in 1933

Edward Kennedy "Duke" Ellington was born in Washington, D.C., the capital of the United States, in 1899. He is known for his piano playing, bandleading, and especially for being one of America's greatest composers.

The type of music Ellington became famous for is called jazz. Jazz is an original American style of music that started right around the time Duke was born. It was invented by African Americans in the city of New Orleans. Jazz started out by taking bits and pieces of many different musical styles. Often, jazz music has a loud brass-band sound that was inspired by marching bands in New Orleans. It usually has an exciting rhythm and powerful expressive feeling that comes from two styles of music: ragtime and blues.

The Jazz Expression, by Victor Haboush

Most importantly, jazz has a sound that comes right from each musician's beliefs and experiences. People found that jazz was great fun to listen to and dance to, and it became very popular.

Edward Kennedy "Duke" Ellington grew up in a loving family. He was very close to his mother. She raised him well and always encouraged him. From his father, Edward learned a lot of manners and how to be stylish and elegant. Mr. Ellington was an experienced butler who had even worked at the White House when Teddy Roosevelt was president.

While he was growing up, Edward was mostly interested in baseball and art. One day, after Edward was accidentally hit in the head with a baseball bat, his mother decided to start him on piano lessons. She thought it would be a much safer activity. Edward, however, didn't care for piano lessons at all as a kid, and his parents finally gave up on him.

It wasn't until he was a teenager that
Edward became interested in the piano.
One day he got a chance to hear a really
great piano player named Harvey Brooks.
Harvey was about the same age as Edward,
and impressed him so much that Edward
decided to give the piano another chance,
right away.

Edward learned to play the piano pretty much on his own. He got advice from talented local piano players, as well as from some who were passing through Washington, D.C., on their way to and from jobs.

Edward wrote and performed one of his earliest songs for a high-school dance. It went over very well. Edward was proud that a song he had written was well liked, and he enjoyed being the center of attention. Even though Edward was interested in becoming an artist and was even offered a scholarship to an important art school, he decided to try and make music his career. He began writing as many new songs as he could.

It was around this time that Edward Kennedy Ellington got his nickname. A friend told him that it was important for popular music composers to have a catchy name. "Duke" seemed to fit Edward because of his stylish and gentlemanly ways. Many famous jazz musicians have had nicknames that describe something about them or their music, like Fats Waller, Jelly Roll Morton, Tricky Sam Nanton, Count Basie, Willie "The Lion" Smith, Louis "Satchmo" Armstrong, Dizzy Gillespie, and many more.

Around 1917, Duke and some of his friends formed a small band called Duke's Serenaders. They played at parties, dances, and clubs all over Washington, D.C. In 1918, Duke got married. He and his wife, Edna, had a son, Mercer, in 1919.

Jazz trumpeter Louis Armstrong (at right), shown here with Duke, was nicknamed "Satchmo,"—a shortened form of "satchel mouth"— because his smile was said to be as big as a large purse!

Jockey Club, a scene of Harlem nightlife in 1929, by Archibald J. Motley, Jr.

Duke knew that in order to make it as a musician, and be able to support his family, he and his friends would have to go to New York City. New York was where all the great jazz bands were playing.

Duke loved the excitement and glamour of New York, especially a section called Harlem.

Harlem was a mainly African American neighborhood where African Americans could live without having to deal as much with being looked down on or treated badly, as they did in most places in the United States at this time. Many black doctors, lawyers, teachers, writers, artists, and musicians moved to Harlem. They created an exciting time in history that became known as the Harlem Renaissance.

13

The Washingtonians in
New York City in 1925

In New York, Duke and some friends from Washington formed a band called The Washingtonians. But it was almost impossible to get a job, because there were so many musicians around. Jazz players from New Orleans, Chicago, and St. Louis heard they could make more money in the dance halls and nightclubs of New York. The Washingtonians keep trying, though, and finally their luck changed. They were hired to play in a well-known nightspot called Barron's Exclusive Club. They did very well, and were soon offered jobs in other popular nightclubs.

Things were going great for Duke, and got even better when a new trumpet player joined the band. His name was James "Bubber" Miley. Before Bubber came into the band, the Washingtonians' music was fairly quiet and moody with some ragtime thrown in once in a while for people to dance to. It wasn't really jazz music, which is what all the nightclubs really wanted.

Not only did Bubber Miley know a lot about jazz, he also made a very special sound with his instrument. Bubber was able to make a growling noise and use a mute to

create a wild kind of sound that few trumpet players had done before or since. A mute is a device attached to a musical instrument to soften or muffle its tone. In the 1920s, a mute was just the end of a bathroom plunger that was put over the end of a horn.

The entrance to Harlem's Cotton Club

Bubber Miley gave Duke's band a wild, hot jazz sound that was much different from other bands of the day. It's easy to hear Bubber's playing in such popular Duke Ellington recordings as "East St. Louis Toodle-oo" and "Black and Tan Fantasy."

By 1927, the Washingtonians had changed their name to the Duke Ellington Orchestra, and were playing at the Cotton Club—the most famous nightclub in New York! Duke began to bring other new members into the band, and was writing one hit song after another.

Duke Ellington (seated at piano) and his band

One thing that made Duke Ellington's band different from just about any other jazz band of the time was that Duke made sure to surround himself with the best musicians he could find—musicians like Bubber Miley— who could make a one-of-a-kind sound with their instruments.

Duke would listen to his members play different parts of the music he wrote until it sounded just right to him. Duke played his band kind of like an instrument, giving his players a chance to do their own special thing.

Duke with drummer
Sonny Greer in 1940

This not only gave Duke's music a unique jazz sound, but made his band members feel good about being an important part of each musical piece.

Another thing Duke did well was to mix the different instrumental sounds in his band. Many jazz experts have compared this to mixing colors—or painting with sound. When you close your eyes and listen to music, you can sometimes picture colors. A cool clarinet sound might remind you of the color blue. A hot sound from a trumpet might remind you of blazing red, and saxophone notes remind some people of liquid gold!

A good example of Duke mixing musical
sound-colors is a piece called "The Mooche."
Because Duke had once been interested
in being an artist, colors were always
important to him. Many of Duke's pieces,
including "Mood Indigo," "Black and Tan
Fantasy," and "Magenta Haze," have colors
in their titles.

Often, Duke and his musicians would have a picture in mind or would be telling a story when they composed or played their music. In one famous piece called "Harlem Airshaft," Duke expressed all the exciting daily activities he saw and heard going on in a Harlem apartment building. When you hear "Harlem Airshaft," it's fun to listen to the different instruments jumping around and changing moods. Duke did this to give his piece the feeling of energy and life in a busy apartment building.

25

By 1940, Duke Ellington had one of the most popular bands in the United States. They made radio broadcasts, records, and appearances all over the country. Unfortunately, in many of the cities where Duke played, there were people who were prejudiced against African Americans. Sometimes Duke and his band had a hard time getting hotel rooms or service in a restaurant. Duke didn't want to put up with that kind of treatment and decided

to travel with his band members in their own private train cars. The railroad would leave Duke's cars parked on an unused track until they were ready to move on. Now Duke and his orchestra could eat, sleep, and live comfortably when they arrived in an unfamiliar and maybe not-so-welcoming town.

As it turned out, Duke loved traveling by train. He got lots of ideas for new songs by listening to the train's sounds as it rolled along, and by looking out over the beautiful scenery as it passed by.

Duke Ellington's music was as popular as ever until the 1950s. Then people started becoming more interested in new types of music, like rock and roll. Duke's style of jazz seemed old-fashioned to many younger people, and some jazz experts thought Duke Ellington's best music was behind him.

Duke writing music

Duke was disappointed, but didn't give up. He worked as hard as ever, writing music and working with his band. Finally, in 1956, something happened that put Duke back on top again.

Duke was invited to play the closing music for a jazz festival in Newport, Rhode Island. It was late at night when Duke and his orchestra came on stage to play. People in the audience were tired and some of them were beginning to go home. Duke knew that in order to get people's attention, he would have to do something pretty special. Duke gave his saxophone player, Paul Gonsalves, the go-ahead to do his best solo during a musical piece called "Diminuendo and Crescendo in Blue."

Saxophonist
Paul Gonsalves

Paul Gonsalves not only did his best, but played one of the greatest saxophone solos in the history of jazz! Duke's plan worked. People in the audience went wild. They started dancing in the aisles and standing on their chairs to cheer. They loved what they were hearing. The next day, newspaper reporters wrote about what had happened.

After the Newport Jazz Festival, Duke and his orchestra were popular once again. For the rest of his life, Duke kept busy writing music and giving concerts all over the world.

Duke Ellington died in 1974. He was one of the first composers to show that jazz could be more than just popular dance music. He showed that jazz could be as beautiful and important as classical music.

Today it's as easy as ever to hear Duke Ellington's wonderful music. It's not hard to find online radio stations that stream his music for free.

LEARN MORE BY TAKING THE
ELLINGTON QUIZ!

(ANSWERS ON THE NEXT PAGE.)

1. Duke Ellington's first piano instructor had an unusual, but well-fitting name for a piano teacher. What was his teacher's name?

   a Marietta Clinkscales
   b Harvey Keypounder
   c Sergey Rocknrollmaninoff

2. **TRUE OR FALSE:**
When Duke Ellington sat down to write a new piece of music, he demanded complete and total quiet.

3. Even though Duke Ellington is considered one of the greatest jazz composers ever, he didn't like to describe his music as jazz. What did Duke prefer to call his music?

   a Space Age music
   b American music
   c Traveling music

4. **TRUE OR FALSE:**
Much to Duke's disappointment, his only son, Mercer, showed no interest at all in music. Mercer went on to become a successful men's suit designer.

5. **TRUE OR FALSE:**
Duke Ellington worked and traveled all the time. One of the things he really looked forward to all year long was a nice quiet vacation in the Caribbean.

6. Duke had a few part-time jobs as a teenager. What job really helped start his musical career?

   a Piano mover
   b Soda jerk
   c Tambourine tester

ANSWERS

1. **a** Duke's Mom hired Marietta Clinkscales to give her son piano lessons. Unfortunately for Marietta, eight-year-old Duke had very little interest in playing the piano, and was often missing when Ms. Clinkscales showed up.

2. **FALSE** Duke Ellington was used to working in all kinds of crazy conditions. It didn't matter if the radio was blasting or phones were ringing. When Duke started out in the music business, he often worked in a large studio, where as many as ten other musicians were pounding out their own piano pieces. Duke learned early on to tune out surrounding noise and concentrate on his own music.

3. **b** Duke Ellington felt that jazz music was established years before his time and stopped using the term to describe his music. Since he was influenced by so many different kinds of music he heard in the United States, he preferred to simply call his style "American Music."

4. **FALSE** Mercer Ellington followed in his father's footsteps. He was an excellent trumpet player and led his own band. Mercer also became the business manager for Duke Ellington and his Orchestra.

5. **FALSE** Duke Ellington never took a vacation. He traveled with his orchestra all over the world, playing almost every day! Duke loved doing that so much he never felt the need for a vacation. His band members felt the same way, too.

6. **b** Duke worked at a soda fountain as a soda jerk. He added carbonated water to ice cream drinks by jerking a lever. Duke was inspired by the rhythm and fizzy sound when he pulled the lever. This led to writing his first musical piece, *Soda Fountain Rag*.